Into Your Hand

Into Your Hand

Confronting Good Friday

Walter Brueggemann

Foreword by
Richard Rohr

scm press

© Walter Brueggemann, 2014, 2015

First published by Cascade Books,
An Imprint of Wipf and Stock Publishers.

This edition published in 2015 by SCM Press

Editorial office
Invicta House,
108–114 Golden Lane
London, EC1Y 0TG

SCM Press is an imprint of Hymns Ancient and Modern Ltd
(a registered charity)
13a Hellesdon Park Road, Norwich, Norfolk, NR6 5DR

www.scmpress.co.uk

British Library Cataloguing in Publication data

A catalogue record for this book is available
from the British Library

978 0 334 05413 9

Printed and bound by
CPI Group (UK) Ltd, Croydon, CR0 4YY

Contents

Foreword

So strange that a Good Friday book would make me so happy! It somehow seems wrong and inappropriate. That was surely not Walter Brueggemann's original intention. Or was it? Maybe even unbeknown to him?

As I read each powerful meditation and perfectly connected psalm, I experienced the healing power that contact with Big Truth will always give. This was not the sentimentalized Good Friday "seven last words" that I had grown up with, but a full body blow of contact with Reality. Making use of the biblical scholarship and sharp insight that we have all come to expect from him, Walter Brueggemann then goes further. He reveals an amazing awareness of human suffering, family, relationships, despair, hard won faith, and personal grief that the crucifixion accounts beautifully and subtly reveal.

If it is true that it is contact with Reality that makes us whole, and if that is the salvific function of the Christ Life, then it is no wonder or surprise that these meditations would make make us very happy indeed. Not only is the confluence of life and death the supreme human paradox, but it also has the power to create a paradox of emotions in the soul. One can be both stricken and deeply joyful at the same time. One can be afflicted and somehow content in the same moment. But only at the level of soul and Spirit! And that is exactly where this magnificent little book will lead you.

Even a little bit of God goes a very long way. Even a little portion of truth satisfies the soul. Even a momentary contact with Reality is enough to stun us into a strange kind of satisfied silence. But in each case it is a suffering to stay there and stand there and allow such an electric shock to the soul. Jesus on the cross, and his words from that place, show us exactly how to stay there. And from that position he also shows us the immense price of solidarity with the suffering of the world, which is also the suffering of God. Then the Marys standing below, mirror the mystery in feminine form, and show us how to stand with all victims without creating more victims ourselves.

Without exaggerating, I know these finely meditated meditations can and will have the same effect on any sincere and serious reader. They will discover you! As true Gospel always does. They will open up parts of your experience and your inner solidarity with divine and human sadness—which might have been too much to "know" until the very moment of reading. That is the patient and polite way that grace always works. That is job of any Scripture that we dare to call "Holy" Scripture. That is the lovely vocation that Walter Brueggemann never tires of. And we, we many, are the always satisfied beneficiaries. Enjoy now the electric shock of happiness—and simultaneous sadness—that Reality always brings!

Fr. Richard Rohr, O.F.M.

Albuquerque, New Mexico
Feast of the Transfiguration, 2014

Preface

THESE SEVEN HOMILIES WERE offered at my home church, St. Timothy Episcopal Church, on Good Friday, 2014. They were part of a three-hour service consisting in music and Scripture reading, the three hours with reference to the time when Jesus was on the cross. I am glad to thank our rector, Roger Greene, and our Music Director and Organist, Philip Clary, for the design of the service, and salute my fellow members at St. Timothy who shared in the service that many of us found to be quite moving.

St. Timothy is a lively suburban church with a vigorous mix of conservative and liberal opinion, but with steadfast commitment to Episcopal order and practice. It is blessed by gifted, attentive clergy, by uncommon musical talent and imagination led by our Music Director and by an engaged attentive congregation that has a sustained missional sensibility. It is accustomed to thoughtful preaching. And it is appreciative of a wide repertoire of music that is well rendered by a mix of lay and professional voices. St. Tim has not, at least in any recent time, had an extended (three-hour) afternoon Good Friday service, usually preferring a Friday night service. This service, nonetheless, was reasonably well attended, with some remaining for all three hours and of course many others coming and going for briefer segments of the service. The congregation is led in a way that pays attention to "spiritual" growth and nurture, so that the pauses of silence in this service were, I think, welcome and not at all awkward. Clearly a three hour service invites such engaged pauses, some covered by music and some left free for the Spirit.

At St. Tim, as elsewhere in our indulgent and (for some) prosperous culture, Good Friday is an odd, abrasive occasion. The preacher and the congregation together face a series of seductions that are powerfully available. One temptation is to skip the day liturgically (and theologically) and to rush to Easter. This is in part, we say, because we do not have time. But beyond the lack of time, we would rush past Good Friday to Easter because we are inured to a triumphalism in which the cross is empty and death is defeated. Thus it is not easy to pause for such a hard encounter that summons us to "the crucified God." Or we are tempted to treat the theological produce of Good Friday in privatistic ways, as though whatever was accomplished on Friday pertained singularly to "me." We did indeed sing, "Were you there?" with its quite private refrain, "It causes *me* to tremble." The "you" is taken as a singular, as though "I" were there at the cross alone. What is missing in such an articulation, of course, is the great momentus social significance of the event that attests the challenge Jesus posed to the Roman Empire and the violent response of the empire to that challenge.

I suppose that we would do better to speak of "the execution" of Jesus rather than "the crucifixion," as the latter term has by now acquired a kind of pious tilt to it that precludes the brutality of the context. And if we privatize to the disregard the Roman Empire, how much more difficult it is to transfer the matter to a critique of contemporary imperial practice, most especially that of the US empire that might readily execute (or "render") such threats. On the other hand, there is a temptation, given current disputes about "substitutionary atonement," to imagine some kind of "magic in the blood" that is shed on Friday. That is not a very deep Episcopal temptation, but I suspect it is everywhere among us as a cultural force. The current move in New Testament scholarship toward "empire studies," as in the work of Richard Horsley, Brigitte Kahl, and Neil Elliott among others, tells against this, but that scholarship has scarcely touched the church yet. And when it does, conventional notions of the salvific impact of the day become more difficult. All of these possible seductions seem to me to make it hard to know exactly what we are doing on Good Friday.

I suggest that we must recognize, as the church has always done in its effort to take the Eucharist seriously, that it is best to stay faithful to the words, but to be careful in imposing meaning, and to give lots of room for interpretation because the verbal witnesses themselves do not specify or require certain meanings. That gives the preacher lots of room in which to work; it also gives the congregation lots of room in which to listen. Truth to tell, the drama of Good Friday, as it is variously given in the gospel traditions, defies explanatory conclusions. The most a preacher can do is to hope to open some access points for fresh reflection.

The modifier "Good" is bound to give us pause. One may legitimately wonder what is good about such a state execution. If we stay with Friday, it is surely a good (whatever we make of salvific outcomes), that Jesus kept his identity and his vocation without any compromise with the executing empire. At a minimum, he is given us as a righteous man who was unjustly executed by an anxious state. His generous faith refused the power of death. We are, of course, permitted to push beyond Friday to Sunday. We know the outcome! The victorious "finish" of Friday also means the theological "finish" of the empire and its power of death. The preacher's task, I take it, is to witness to this "good" in contemporary life, to insist in ways that do not jar conventional piety too much, that the good of gospel fidelity both exposes and defeats the combination of raw power and greedy confiscation that now marks our economy and our public life. That good, embodied in the vulnerable person of Jesus, is enacted in forgiveness, yields nothing to evil, and eventually rests safely in the hands of God who, in the narrative, outlasts the force of death.

Thus at St. Tim and elsewhere Good Friday is not in a vacuum. And many congregants tracked and participated in the full liturgic flow of Hoy Week. This included a Taize service with Eucharist, a Jewish Passover meal (as much as Gentiles understand it), a Thursday foot washing and stripping of the altar, and then a joyous Saturday night Easter vigil followed by a generous party of food and celebration, and finally Easter services. Such a sequence here and elsewhere characterizes the execution as a way-station of abandonment that is not an endpoint of abandonment. The requirement is to pause long enough—whether three hours is long enough is unclear—to see that the abandonment is a genuine abandonment. I suspect, with our endlessly connected electronic life to sense real abandonment is not easy, especially if abandonment is more than a monetary dead zone for cells. This dead zone is indeed a zone of death, and the preacher must try to convey that.

Our service not only featured a rich variety of musical offerings, but for each "word" we heard read a psalm. Happily our clergy did not do "snippets" of psalms as is sometimes done, but we heard whole psalms so that we could traverse the long journey of presence and absence in the Psalms. Most of these psalm selections are obvious choices. I suppose the least obvious usage is the selection of Psalm 127, which, in patriarchal fashion, celebrates "a quiver full of sons." The psalm seems appropriate with my accent on the "family forming" work of Jesus. As Good Friday does not happen in a vacuum but comes in the sequence of Holy Week, so the "words" of the cross do not occur in a vacuum, but belong in the long practice of the church's singing of the Psalms. The effect of hearing complete psalms along with these "words" is to make available a very thick practice in which we can participate. Some of the connections to the psalms are more obvious than others, but each of the psalms helps to situate the "words of Jesus" in the actual life of Israel.

I had in previous time done a "word" or two in Good Friday services, but never the full complement of seven. I found it hard work to prepare for the service, but very satisfying hard work. Because I have no particular expertise in New Testament texts, I did not linger very long over critical matters, though I hope I am informed enough not to commit gross violation. I have come to think, increasingly, that the task of preaching is simply to give the congregation access to the text, and the text, led by the spirit, will do much of its own work. It follows from that that I am not too much inclined to do explanatory work about context, though a general consensus on current study is useful, not least concerning "empire studies."

On the other hand, I think increasingly that the preacher does not need to work very hard at contemporeneity or contemporary "application" of the text if the text is well voiced. Partly that is because contemporeneity pours out of the text; but partly it is because contemporary connections are not persuasive unless the congregant is permitted to see them and make the connections for herself. It is invariably the case that the text is more interesting and more compelling than most of what we are able to say about it. What I have tried to do, thus, is to treat these texts in ways that will let the congregation do its own Good Friday work.

The scandal of "the execution" still leaves us to ponder its "goodness." It is hard to see how that goodness could possibly have a decisive say or impact in a technological world of mobile capital in which the holiness of God and the validity of the neighbor have become marginal matters at best. It is difficult to imagine that this "good" could prevail in our world, and so we are permitted, I think, traces of despair, cynicism, and resignation. But, of course, that is how it was on that first Friday that came to be called "good." The power of death, in its many worldly manifestations, is always too strong. To take three hours to ponder this on Friday, however, is to entertain the thought that the Goodness of the occasion is not a slight possibility to be squeezed into a drama in which old power prevails. Good Friday and all that it performs is an insistence that its claims will not in any way accommodate the business as usual of old power. Rather one starts at a different place and refuses business as usual from the ground up. That is surely what Jesus did on that day. That clearly is what the gospel writers intend. And that clearly is what preacher and congregation propose to do on this day that refuses accommodation. This service sounds acute testimony to a steadfast refusal of all old certitudes.

I thank K. C. Hanson and his cohorts at Cascade Books, yet again, for their willingness to produce the book and for getting these sermons into a book so promptly. I

Preface

am grateful to my good friend Richard Rohr for his timely foreword. And I give thanks for St. Timothy Church for sustaining this liturgical script of our life.

Walter Brueggemann

Columbia Theological Seminary

August 1, 2014

1

Father, Forgive Them, for They Know not What They Do

(Luke 23:34; Psalm 103)

DID YOU KNOW THAT this famous verse, "Father, forgive them for they know not what they do," is missing from some of the most important manuscripts of the New Testament? That it is missing in some manuscripts means it is treated with suspicion by some scholars, whether it belongs there and if he really said it . . . plus that it is not reported in any Gospel narrative except Luke.

You could ask a question about what the absence of this verse means in two ways. Assume that Jesus said it: why would the early church leave it out and pretend that he did not say it? Well, maybe they found it too radical. Maybe they figured that there was a limit to forgiveness and if there is, then that red line was surely crossed in the execution of Jesus. If there is something that could not be forgiven, this must be it, well beyond an acceptable limit. In the narrative, those who wanted him dead, those who shouted, "Crucify him" knew that they will carry blood-guilt that is beyond forgiveness. There is good reason that Jesus could not ask forgiveness for that. So it is missing in some reliable manuscripts.

But turn the question around. What if he did not say it for those reasons, but they put it in some manuscripts anyway, even if it does not belong there? I think it is there because the early church could not imagine the narrative without it. So they had him say it, even if he did not. They could not imagine that Jesus did not say it, because the word of forgiveness is his ultimate, most radical word, and it must not be left unspoken, even if he did not say it. So it is there! In Luke's narrative, moreover, it is the very first thing he says when he arrives at this place of his execution. It is as though he seizes the initiative and wants to frame his execution in a specific way by making this prayer at the outset. Before you do anything of the process of execution, know my attitude toward you. Know that I will not hold a grudge against you. I will forgive you who do the actual killing. I will forgive the authorities who do not even come to Calvary but who have engineered the killing. I will forgive you because it is my most elemental propensity to forgive. It is my signature act, that for which I am best and most faithfully known.

But Jesus himself does not forgive them. Maybe he is too busy, or that it is too big a task for him. He refers the matter to his Father. He says, "Father, forgive them." He addresses his petition to the creator of heaven and earth, to the Lord of all that is, seen and unseen. He draws the attention of the Father to his particular moment, to these particular offenders, to his particular moment of suffering and death. It is as though this act of forgiveness has cosmic proportion, as forgiveness always does. The extremity of his situation is matched by the extremity and urgency of the prayer. He asks of the father an outrageous act of self-giving, for who among us wants to forgive the killers of our beloved son or daughter? But Jesus knows the heart of the Father who is at bottom a forgiver.

Jesus is nurtured in the ancient Psalm that recites God's overpowering, relentless resolve to heal the world:

> Do not forget all his benefits—
> > who forgives all your iniquity,
> who heals all your diseases,
> > who redeems your life from the Pit,
> who crowns you with steadfast love and mercy,
> > who satisfies you with good as long as you live.
> > (Psalm 103:2–5)

This is an amazing inventory of what the Father God does: forgive, heal, redeem, crown, satisfy; they are all synonyms. They are all actions that correct the deficiencies of the world, because the Father wills the world to well-being. These are God's characteristic and recurring actions, and the first one is "forgive"! And then the Psalmist can say in confidence:

> He will not always accuse,
> > nor will he keep his anger forever.
> He does not deal with us according to our sins,
> > nor repay us according to our iniquities . . .
> As far as the east is from then west,
> > so far he removes our transgressions from us.
> As a father has compassion for his children
> > so the LORD has compassion for those who fear
> > him.
> He knows how we were made;
> > he remembers that we are dust. (vv. 9–14)

God does not retain anger. God does not hold grudges. God does not keep score. God's proper business is compassion. And that compassion is in response to who we are. God knows, from Genesis 2, that we are dust . . . feeble, frail, weak, inadequate. So God compensates, making up for what we will not do ourselves.

Jesus stands in sharp contrast to those who mock him who will kill him. They are busy, task-oriented, prone to violence, cynical, greedy for gain. He is not:

- he has no task to perform, confident of the Father; he doesn't need to do anything,

- he is an agent of non-violence;

- he is not greedy for anything;

- he has no cynicism.

If we focus on that contrast between Jesus and those around him, there are here two ways in the world, the way of suffering love and the way of anxious violence. The narrative invites us to choose.

The Father does not answer the prayer soon. The answer that leaps to forgiveness is at Easter. God's forgiveness at Easter makes it the decisive moment in the history of the world. In Easter God has no vengeance, no grudge, no retaliation, only a reach into the hate and death of the world to make all things new. We live in the wake of that sweeping action. So when you hear in the liturgy, "Christ is risen; he is risen indeed," mark that as an answer to this prayer, as forgiveness. The world is forgiven. The men of hate and violence are forgiven. The greedy, cruel executioners are forgiven. The pattern of death is broken. This is not a Friday moment, but it is a Sunday answer to the Friday prayer.

So here is a take-away for us. The drama of Friday is changed by this remarkable prayer of generosity. The drama of our lives is changed by the self-giving of Jesus and the reach of the Father. The drama of the world is made new by the forgiveness of the Father. We need not carry old grudges or old guilts, because the Father has no interest in them. The world is driving itself to death. But the reach of Jesus has broken that cycle of destruction. It only remains to act it out. Bishop Tutu and his daughter Mpho, in their new book on forgiveness, write:

> When I develop a mindset of forgiveness, rather than a mindset grievance, I don't just forgive a particular act; I become a more forgiving person. With a grievance mindset, I look at the world and see all that is wrong. When I have a forgiveness mindset, I start to see the world not through grievance but through gratitude. In other words, I look at the world and start to see what is right. There is a special kind of magic that happens when I become a more forgiving person—it is quite remarkable. What was once a grave affront melts into nothing more than a thoughtless or careless act. What was once a reason for rupture and alienation becomes an opportunity for repair and greater intimacy. A life that seemed littered with obstacles and antagonism is suddenly filled with opportunity and love.[1]

---

1. Desmond Tutu and Mpho Tutu, *The Book of Forgiving: The Fourfold Path for Healing Ourselves and Our World* (New York: HarperOne, 2014) 218–19.

2

Truly I Tell You, Today You Will Be with Me in Paradise
(Luke 23:43; Psalm 27)

OF THE SEVEN STATEMENTS by Jesus on the cross, six of them he just blurts out. This one is unlike those other six, because this one is a response to something that has been said to him. As a result, we must start with the address made to him. The conversation at Golgotha was between two other criminals who were also crucified. The Roman empire did it wholesale! Empires love capital punishment! One of the two, in his anger and fear, taunts Jesus: "Save yourself and us" . . . or maybe you are not really the Messiah. He only wanted not to die. But the other criminal, who was also about to be executed, scolds the first guy. He can see at glance that Jesus, in contrast to the two of them, is an innocent man being unfairly sent to his death.

After he rebukes the other criminal, he addresses Jesus whom he has recognized as an innocent victim. He said to him, "Remember me when you come into your kingdom." He not only sees that Jesus is innocent. He acknowledges who Jesus is. He does not doubt that Jesus has a future beyond his execution. He knows that Jesus will have a "kingdom," that is, a mighty zone of governance. He believes in Jesus, whereas the other criminal doubted his capacity to save.

The man wants to be "remembered." This is not just hope of being recognized and legitimated as a person. He may imagine that when Jesus comes to power (as he surely will), he will issue an amnesty, and he wants to be on the list of those whom he will pardon. He hopes for himself by testifying that Jesus will have a future.

Jesus makes a quite remarkable response to the guy. He affirms to him that he does indeed have a future that the Roman Empire cannot deny him. We may notice three elements in the response of Jesus. First, he says, "Today." Right now! You do not even have to wait for Easter. "Today." Maybe that means when we die, which will be very soon. But maybe it means right now, as soon as I say this to you. The "today" is an incredible welcome, no questions asked, no qualifying exam. Come on in!

Second, Jesus, according to Luke, uses the curious word "paradise." This is a very rare word in the New Testament and is exactly in Greek as it is in English, "paradise." One other use in the New Testament links the word to "the tree of life" (Revelation 2:7), so we take it as an allusion to the Garden of Eden that contained the tree of life. Jesus invites the man back into the garden of well-being that we know in Genesis, before there was violence or alienation. We often suspect, in our common use, that "paradise" means "heaven." But there is no evidence that this concerns "life after death"; paradise is rather a zone of well-being presided over by Jesus, marked by blessedness, fruitfulness, abundance, security, and well-being, all of that on offer right now, today, for the person who trusts Jesus.

But it is the third term that clarifies both "today" and "paradise." "Today you will be with me in paradise" is transposed by Jesus. Now it is not a place but a relationship, it concerns being "with me." The place of well-being, abundance, and blessedness is in relationship to Jesus, in his presence. And that may happen right now, immediately. This welcome offer is this assurance; being with Jesus is a safe place of goodness.

Psalm 27 is an anticipation of this welcome and assurance. The psalmist can say that he is confident even amid trouble:

> When evildoers assail me
>> to devour my flesh—
> my adversaries and foes—
>> they shall stumble and fall.
> Though an army encamp against me,
>> my heart shall not fear;
> though war rise up against me,
>> yet I will be confident. (vv. 2–3)

And then the psalm turns from threat to well-being in the presence of God:

> One thing I asked of the LORD,
>> that will I seek after;
> to live in the house of the LORD
>> all the days of my life,
> to behold the beauty of the LORD,
>> and to inquire in his temple. (v. 4)

The one thing for this psalmist is to see the beauty of God's presence. And then the psalm ends with a great affirmation:

9

> I believe that I shall see the goodness of the LORD
>> in the land of the living.
> Wait for the LORD;
>> be strong, and let your heart take courage;
>> wait for the LORD! (vv. 13–14)

These words could have been on the lips of the man who addresses Jesus with "remember me." The psalm anticipates the "land of the living." He is so confident of Jesus that he can picture himself in the land of the living, welcomed there by the ruler of that land of life. Rome by contrast is the land of dying, the land of killing, the land of leaving behind.

The exchange of Jesus with the man, anticipated in the psalm, is in the context of the land of death, a context of violence, shouting soldiers, hammering custodians with nails, restlessness among the crowd, crap shooting for his clothes, a busy place where there is no hope. Their conversation occurs in this land of death. It is like the land we inhabit. More guns, more rape of women, more torture, more food-stamp cuts, more environmental disaster, more corruption, more exploitation, more injustice, more greed in the corporate world, more deception in the church world, more manipulation in the government world, all marks of the land of death.

And in the midst of it, there is this bid for welcome and a response that defies the world of death. Death will not win. Because Jesus has invested his life against it. And the other man knows it. When he sees Jesus, he knows that God's will for life is stronger than death. He knows that forgiveness will outrun violence. He knows that generosity will beat fear and hate. He knows that paradise is any place where the presence of Jesus prevails; and he can dwell there.

We dare imagine Jesus saying the same thing to us if and when we recognize him for who he is:

Truly I Tell You, Today You Will Be with Me in Paradise

- Today . . . right now;
- Paradise, a zone of covenantal well-being;
- With me, with Jesus, welcomed into the zone of compassion.

Now and in the hour of our death, we are unafraid. So the Psalmist can say:

> The LORD is my light and my salvation;
>> whom shall I fear?
> The LORD is the stronghold of my life;
>> of whom shall I be afraid? (v. 1)

3

Woman, Here Is Your Son;
Here is Your Mother

(John 19:26–27; Psalm 127)

THIS IS THE FIRST time, in the Fourth Gospel, that Jesus speaks from the cross. His statement is a surprise in context, for we have just been told about the mocking abuse of the soldiers. But as John tells it, Jesus is not preoccupied with that abuse. His attention is elsewhere. The scene juxtaposes the *aggressive soldiers*, epitome of the empire that executes him, and the cadre of *weeping, helpless women* who keep vigil at his execution. This dramatic contrast of empire and vulnerable vigil of women is an invitation for us to position ourselves in the narrative.

That group keeping vigil includes the two other Marys and his mother. She remains unnamed and is present nowhere else in John's Gospel. The three women are there in their grief along with "the disciple whom he loved." The narrative suggests that Jesus is preoccupied with his mother and tends to unfinished family business as she is left vulnerable and alone in a patriarchal society.

The words of Jesus are "family forming." He makes a connection between his mother and his disciple, and by his words declares them to have a new, familial relationship. It is as though he makes formal introductions: Mother, meet your new son; meet your new mother. He creates a new mother–son relationship. What is left unsaid but obvious is that he, her proper son, will not be present in the family configuration. He will be lost, remembered but absent, not the son who can make a difference to her. We have seen, from the other gospels, that Jesus is abandoned by God on the cross. Now his mother is abandoned and he takes steps to override her abandonment by making sure she has a son who can look after her. Psalm 127 reminds us of how important sons are in that society:

> Sons are indeed a heritage from the LORD,
>> the fruit of the womb a reward.
> Like arrows in the hand of a warrior
>> are the sons of one's youth.
> Happy is the man who has
>> his quiver full of them.
> He shall not be put to shame
>> when he speaks with his enemies in the gate.
> (vv. 3–5)

Having a son matters hugely in that patriarchal world! Now she has lost her son. But Jesus has provided a new son for her.

We are left to interpret his quick scene. I thought of two angles. First, we may take the narrative at face value. In a patriarchal society a son has an obligation to his mother, especially as his father is nowhere in the picture. Jesus is a family man, and one could parse this exchange toward "family values." Jesus cares for his mother. The narrative ends with this assurance: "From that hour he took her into his own home." It is only after he secures a new home for his mother with a new son that Jesus can, in his account, think of himself and his thirst.

But things are never as they seem in John's gospel. So we may imagine that there is a strong current of church theology beyond the obvious family note. This amazing narrative mention of his mother may reflect a beginning of a church tendency to lift up Mary, mother of Jesus, as a reference point in faith. Luke began his story of Jesus with Mary and her Magnificat. Now John ends his story with a reference to her, to assure that he really has a fleshly mother. Later on the church will designate her "mother of God," though not here yet. Already in John 9:38, John reports that one "worshipped him." So the gospel is on its way to a very high theology that will enhance Mary. On the other hand, reference to the disciple who became her son, no doubt John, is an anticipation that in time to come John will become foremost among the apostles in the church. This is church theology as the gospel looks beyond Calvary to the church after Easter. In that sense, this narrative looks to how life will be after Easter with an enhanced mother and a beloved disciple who together constitute a new evangelical way in the world.

But what strikes me is this. His execution destroyed his family as executions by empires always do. He had to make a new family. He makes a new family by designating mother and son between the two, Mary and the disciple, who in fact are not kin. The clue, perhaps, is that this is the disciple whom he loved. The word "love" in John's gospel is always a loaded term. It has to do with complete self-giving to another. Thus "God so loved the world." And then Jesus gives his disciples a new commandment, "Love one another." Jesus loved this disciple. He loved him as the disciple who had fully embraced the command of Jesus. He embraced what Jesus had intended.

This suggests that the new family that Jesus makes is not made of blood connections, but of love connection that overrides all old kinship connection. In the Gospel of Mark, very different to be sure, they told Jesus,

> Your mother and your brothers and sisters are outside, asking for you. (Mark 3:32)

And he answered them:

> Who are my mother and my brothers . . . Here are my mother and brothers! Whoever does the will of God is my brother and sister and mother. (vv. 33–35)

The new family that Jesus is forming is a family of those who embrace God's will and purpose which is the purpose of love and peace and justice. The making of this new family suggests that we should not be so deeply set in old family ways with their old tribal habits and old treasured convictions and old tired ideologies and biases. The Messiah who makes new families calls us out to meet new brothers and sisters, new mothers and fathers, new sons and daughters. His words of family-making for this new mother and this new son may have been a surprise to Mary and to the disciple. They continue to surprise us as we are called always to new family that violates all old boundaries of exclusion and defensiveness.

4

My God, My God,
Why Have You Forsaken Me?
(Matthew 27:46; Mark 15:34; Psalm 22)

IF YOU LOOK AT Hymn #636 in the hymnal, "How Firm a
Foundation," you will find the last verse this way:

> The soul that to Jesus hath fled for repose,
> I will not, I will not desert to its foes;
> That soul, though all hell should endeavor to shake,
> I'll never, no never, no never forsake.

We like to sing such reassuring words of God's unfailing
loyalty to us. We celebrate it and count on it.

But this Friday throws Jesus' words into the teeth of
that claim. On the cross on that Friday, Matthew and Mark
tell us that this is his final word:

> My God, my God, why have you forsaken me?

And they tell it in Aramaic so that we do not miss the point
that it is a verbatim from his lips.

Popular, easy, reassuring religion imagines God's constant attentiveness to us. But we know better. We know that to live in God's world is to live being abandoned, to face free-fall and absence and aloneness that go all the way to the bottom of reality. This Friday cry of Jesus calls us to relearn abut faith and obedience and discipleship.

Jesus is not the first one to know about being forsaken. He quotes a Psalm. Old Israel knew, well before Jesus, about being abandoned by the God in whom they trusted. And Jesus is not the last one to know about this abandonment. Some of you know it acutely. And beyond our own privileged existence amid our superpower, there are folks in our society and around the world who know of God's abandonment that must not be glossed over. Our TV screens are filled with images of the abandoned . . . distended bodies of the hungry, endless rounds of violence, the poor left behind. Indeed, Isaiah can have God say to old Israel:

> For a brief moment I abandoned you,
>> but with great compassion I will gather you.
> In overflowing wrath for a moment
>> I hid my face from you,
> but with everlasting love I will have compassion on you
>> says the LORD, your Redeemer. (Isaiah 54:7–8)

This Friday is the day we reflect on God-abandonment. We do it for the three hours of darkness on Friday as he lingered on the cross, executed by the state. We linger over it all of Saturday, for there is no reassurance on that day. We do it and notice that the life of Jesus in obedience is a life without resource or reassurance. So I invite you to dwell in abandonment until the Easter vigil. Fix attention on your own abandonment. And if you do not know of it, then fix on someone else who is in abandonment, some of our friends, some of our enemies, all of us Friday people.

But here are some things to notice about this Friday abandonment:

- Jesus was not silent about it; he did not knuckle under in despair or resignation. He cried out with a loud voice. He did not just cry out, "Why have you abandoned me?" He cried out in a loud voice, "My God, my God." He addressed the God who was absent. He summoned God. He insisted that God must come to deliver. The most elemental act of faith is an imperative that insists that on God, that calls God out of absence.

- Jesus was not silent about his abandonment. He lined out his trouble as we may line out the trouble of our world. Many think that as he quotes the first verse of the Psalm, he implies the rest of the Psalm. The Psalm voices to God the wretchedness of life in abandonment:

> Many bulls encircle me,
>> strong bulls of Bashan surround me;
> they open wide their mouths against me,
>> like a ravening and roaring lion . . .
> For dogs are all around me;
>> a company of evildoers encircle me.
> My hands and feet have shriveled;
>> I can count all my bones;
> They stand and gloat over me.
> (vv. 12–13, 16–17)

He was heard in his loud cry! If he did not cry, he would not be heard. He cried out with a loud voice. And then he is able to say:

> From the horns of the wild oxen you have
> rescued me. (v. 21)

- But Mark goes further. He says that as Jesus gave a loud cry,

> The curtain of the temple was torn in two,
> from top to bottom. (Mark 15:38)

The curtain in the temple was the secret mystery of the temple that provided cover for the imperial economy of exploitation. In this moment the cozy relation of religion and state and the corporate economy was shattered. It was exposed as a fraud, broken open by the piercing cry of the forsaken Messiah. It turns out that the cross is no palliative for safe, little religion. It is an upheaval that shatters all the institutional assurances that we treasure, and the holiness of God is left raw in the world.

- But Mark goes further. At the end of the paragraph he reports that the Roman soldier who was assigned guard duty at the cross said, almost too late,

> Truly this man was God's son. (15:39)

This is a staggering acknowledgement by the empire that the superpower with its wealth and power and violence cannot have the final word in the world. It is a moment of daring awareness that the world does not work as superpower or as empire. It works, rather, in raw holiness acted out by agents of foolishness of whom Jesus is the foremost. In this moment the empire knows that weakness will break power, that obedience will shatter complacency. The soldier saw that the honesty of the cross breaks phony assurances given by voices of fraudulent entitlement. He heard in this forsaken loud cry an utterance of truth that exposes his safe world.

- Eventually the Psalm moves to celebrative praise:

> I will tell of your name to my brothers
> and sisters;
> in the midst of the congregation I will
> praise you . . .

> From you comes my praise in the
> great congregation;
> my vows I will pay before those who
> fear him (vv. 22, 25).

And we will do that praise . . . at Easter. But not too soon! We have many hours of forsakenness before that. These are hours in which we may reflect on phony assurances all around us, on institutional deceptions, on the truth of our lives before the holiness of God. The loud cry will turn to glad praise. But before that, it is a loud cry. It is a loud cry for all the abandoned. It is a loud cry that will tear the curtain behind which is no wizard, but only the God of holiness who defeats empire by weakness.

5

I Thirst
(John 19:28; Psalm 42)

As I learned to drink Diet Coke much too often, my mother never failed to say in a firm, gentle voice, "You know, water would quench your thirst much better." My mother was inviting me to a most elemental issue of faith, namely, what are your real thirsts and in what phony thirsts do you indulge? This is a very old question for Christians, going back at least to Augustine who reflected on the ways in which false desires substitute for our real desire for God. This is an immediately contemporary question in our over-indulgent consumer society in which we are endlessly summoned into many false desires and urged, as the TV ad has it, to "Stay thirsty, my friend," and invitation that appeals only to those who have never recognized their real hunger.

I

Jesus on the cross was thirsty. John tells us that the reason he was thirsty was only to match up with the ancient tradition of Psalm. But clearly Jesus, in John's gospel, is a real human being, come in the flesh, who had a real thirst for water. After all, he had been detained by the authorities, interrogated all night in an abusive environment, and then subjected to what must have been a hot Friday sun. He did not need old scripture to advise him to be thirsty. He was a man in need. And of course that they gave him sour wine (more abuse!?). The transaction exhibits a complete mismatch between his thirst and their offer. They needed my mother to tell them, "Water would quench his thirst better." Friday is the day that God subjected God's own self, in the flesh of Jesus, to the reality of elemental, bodily need. That fact helps us to see that this Friday performance is no pretend job. This is a real human person, debased by the force of empire, being denied what he needs, because such empires of power are likely to use extreme measures to maintain their security in the face of real or imagined threats.

II

But of course the Bible, in its vigorous imagination, passes easily from literal, concrete water to figurative water as a way of speaking about the "water of life." Thus our Psalm for this hour, Psalm 42, can begin:

> As the deer longs for flowing streams,
> so my soul longs for you, O God.
> My soul thirsts for God,
> for the living God. (Psalm 42:1)

This is a deep thirst for God. This is a thirst to be connected to the source of all of life, to be gladly dependent upon God, to be grateful to God, to be receptive to God's gifts and God's presence. The Psalmist lines out a yearning for God, but also an absence of God, and a deep discouragement that results from such absence. The most amazing part of the Psalm is that it fully acknowledges what being cut off from God is like, with a cast down self:

> My tears have been my food day and night,
>> while people say to me continually, "Where is your God?" (v. 3)

But the Psalmist does not leave us there. The refrain of the Psalm is a summons beyond despair and back to God:

> Why are you cast down, O my soul,
>> and why are you disquieted within me?
> Hope in God; for I shall again praise him,
>> my help and my God. (v. 5)

That refrain is repeated in verse 11:

> Why are you cast down, O my soul
>> and why are you disquieted within me?
> Hope in God; for I shall again praise him,
>> my help and my God. (v. 11)

The words come yet again in the next Psalm:

> Why are you cast down, O my soul,
>> and why are you disquieted within me"
> Hope in God; for I shall again praise him
>> my help and my God. (Psalm 43:5)

The Psalmist trusts that unquenched thirst is not the last word. The thirst will be quenched. Because God is faithful. So the Psalmist can remember going to church to the presence of God:

> These things I remember
>> as I pour out my soul,

how I went with the throng,

and led them in the procession to the house of
God,

with glad shouts and songs of thanksgiving,

a multitude keeping festival. (Psalm 42:4)

More than that, the Psalmist can anticipate future partici-
pation in worship. The dry spell can be short term, because
the water of life is available. Thus in the next Psalm:

Then I will go to the altar of God,

to God my exceeding joy;

and I will praise you with the harp,

O God, my God. (Psalm 43:4)

Later on Ezekiel can anticipate that the very water of life will
flow out for under the altar of the temple in Jerusalem. In
Christian tradition, this is surely a reference to the Eucharist.

III

On this Friday as we ponder Jesus' unrequited thirst, we
move back and forth between the literal and the figurative
concerning water. As our thirst is figurative, remember
Jesus and the woman at the well:

Everyone who drinks of this water will be thirsty
again, but those who drink of the water that I
will give them will never be thirsty. The water
that I will give will become in them a spring of
water gushing up to eternal life. The woman said
to him, "Sir, give me this water, so that I may
never be thirsty or have to keep coming here to
draw water." (John 4:13–15)

We are invited to slough off drink that does not quench and get to the living water in the gospel. But then let the thirst be literal. As you know, in the Gospel of Matthew he reprimanded his obdurate critics:

> I was hungry and you gave me no food,
>> I was thirsty and you gave me nothing to drink.
>> (Matthew 25:42)

But he said to the blessed:

> Come, you that are blessed by my Father, inherit the kingdom prepared for you from the foundation of the world; for I was hungry and you gave me food, I was thirsty and you gave me something to drink. I was a stranger and you welcomed me, I was naked and you gave me clothing, I was sick and you took care of me, I was in prison and you visited me. (vv. 34–35)

Think what water you must have to live. Think what unquenching drink you like too much. Think who needs water in our world. And with whom you may share water. And from whom you have withheld water. Think what it means to live in an economy that uses up so much of the world's water with our industry and our military and our waste. And let it ring in our ears, "As you did it to the least, you did it to me."

On Friday, Jesus is reduced to the least, to the most helpless, to the one without recourse or authority. He thirsts. And so do we! And so does our neighbor!

6

It Is Finished!
(John 19:30; Psalm 93)

LONG-TIME FANS OF PROFESSIONAL basketball will remember the old Boston Celtics. They were a very successful team with Bill Russell and Bob Cousey, with John Havileck as the sixth man. And you will remember their spectacular coach, Red Auerbach. He developed a quite dramatic way of coaching, including his "victory cigar." When coach was sure his team was going to win, he would very ostentatiously light up a cigar on the Celtic bench. It was a gesture of some macho assertion, and a quiet way of taunting the opposition. Auerbach had a way of seeing when he would win, and sometimes he lit up his victory cigar quite early, even though the game still had a while to run. And he never miscalculated about his "victory cigar."

Well, the last word Jesus speaks on the cross in John's Gospel is, "It is finished." This is not a statement of defeat or resignation. It is rather God's victory cigar. Already on that Friday, before Easter Sunday, Jesus declared his victory. His work is done. So John can write, "After this, when

Jesus knew that all was now finished . . ." He has done that for which his life was destined. It was a victory for the purposes of God, even if his execution on the cross at the hands of the Roman Empire seemed for the moment like a visible defeat. He knew better! And said so!

I

I want to tell you about that victory accomplished on that Friday. The phrase, "It is finished," is a deliberate allusion back to God's "finish" three times in the Old Testament:

- In Genesis 2, after six days of creation when the earth was made fruitful and blessed, "God finished." At sundown on the sixth day, God saw that it was very good and said, "It is finished!" God has overcome chaos and so God rested as the new king of creation.

- In Exodus 40, after Moses had spent long tedious chapters designing and building the tabernacle for divine presence, Moses could say of his work on the tabernacle, "It is finished." He had provided a resting place for the new king.

- In Joshua 19, when the land of promise had been carefully distributed among the twelve tribes, Joshua could report that the land settlement was completed. It is finished!

Thus "finish" is used for three great achievements of God in Israel's memory:

- the finish of creation and the defeat of chaos;

- the finish of the tabernacle and the defeat of absence;

- the finish of the promised land and the defeat of homelessness.

All of these finishes report on God's great work. Each time God lights a victory cigar to declare the new surge of well-being made possible by a blessed creation, by a tabernacle of presence, and by a safe, secure homeland.

And now a finish of one more victory on Friday. One more achievement by God. One more gift to the world. What is now finished is the victory of God's way in the world enacted by Jesus. Jesus has practiced the way of suffering love, of compassion, mercy, forgiveness, and generosity. On that Friday, the power of death has done its best, and it could not overcome the power of God in the person of Jesus.

- The Friday victory is the defeat of the power of death. The power of death shows up in all the ways that seek to talk us out of our God-given life of well-being. That power shows up in hostility and violence. It shows up in pettiness and selfishness. It shows up in greed and debilitating anxiety. But it is now robbed of its power, because Jesus has prevailed.

- The Friday victory is the defeat of the Roman Empire and all empires (including ours) that depend on muscle and militarism. Jesus has been on trial before the Roman governor Pilate. But he has not given in and has not been found guilty. And now Rome has executed him as an enemy of the state; but it has no power to destroy his love for the world.

- The Friday victory is a defeat for all those who colluded among his own people who thought they could compromise and manipulate their way to well-being. And now, it is finished! It is all finished! It is as if God's victory cigar has been lit up in the third quarter. The power of death will continue compete for a while. But it has lost; it is finished!

II

So let me tell you what it means for us if we note and acknowledge and take seriously that defeat of the power of death:

- It means that the sting of death is gone. We need not fear being diminished any more.

- It means that the power of guilt has evaporated and we need not carry old wounds of shame, because all of that is voided.

- It means that we need no longer operate out of fear and loss or defeat.

- It means that in God's strange new world coming at us, our fundamental worth and dignity are not in jeopardy and we do not need to crawl to the top of anything. We do not even need to be right and have our way.

- It means that we need not use our energy on ourselves, our status or security, but we are free to get our mind off ourselves to notice that the transformative power of God has been let loose all around us, swirling us into the work of justice for the neighbor.

- It means that the neighbor looms front and center for us, for the new rule of Jesus always calls to care for the other in transformative ways.

It is no wonder for this day that we sing Psalm 93, all about the kingship of God, for in this victory we see new rule coming into being before our very eyes:

> The LORD is king; he is robed in majesty;
> > the LORD is robed, he is girded with strength.

He has established the world;
> it shall never be moved;

Your throne is established from of old;
> you are from everlasting. (Psalm 93:1–2)

The Psalm is one more victory cigar for God!

Before Jesus finishes in the Gospel of John, he will say three urgent things to his disciples:

- He will appear to them on Easter and will say to them, "**Peace be with you**" (John 20:19). Do not be wrapped up in anxiety; be at peace!

- He will summon his disciples to "**Feed my sheep**," (John 21:17), care for the vulnerable.

- He will command his disciples, "**Follow me**" (John 21:19). Do what I do! Go where you had not thought to go. Go where your mom and dad with their old fears did not want you to go.

Notice the victory cigar. Notice the victory. In this moment of victory, all the pain is being turned into joy (John 16:20).

7

Father, into Your Hand
I Commend My Spirit

(Luke 23:46; Psalm 31)

TWICE IN THE GOSPEL of Luke Jesus on the cross addresses words to "Father." He speaks first on the cross, "Father, forgive them for they know not what they do." Now in his final word in the narrative of Luke, he cries in a loud voice:

> Father into thy hand I commend my spirit.

He trusts his very life to the Father, the creator of all that is, seen and unseen. His life had derived from the Father, and now he gives his life back to the Father. This close linkage of the Son to the Father will eventually be filled out by the lyrical confession of the church, "God from God, Light from Light, true God from true God," but not yet in Luke. Here it is full trust and obedience, and confidence in the Father, so much confidence that he can relinquish readily to the Father.

We are familiar with the phrase, "I commend my spirit." But we should not overly "spiritualize" this familiar statement. If we push behind the Greek to the old Hebrew tradition, the term "spirit" is also the term for "breath." When we let the term mean spirit/breath, it may turn out, I give my breath back to you, because in that ancient world it was easily understood that breath is a gift from God. You cannot hold your breath very long; you do not possess it. It is a gift given and given and given, as we inhale and exhale. That statement of relinquishment by Jesus is followed, moreover, by the report, "Having said this, he breathed his last." He had relinquished his breath, his very claim to life, back to the Father. We must not, with the familiar language of "spirit," imagine this is a claim for immortality, as though his "spirit" was with God; it is exactly the opposite. His readiness to give up his breath is a readiness to die. He will die willingly, handing his life back to God who gave him breath. He remained, until that final moment, fully in charge of his life; in that moment, he ceases to be in charge and trusts himself to God. His life (breath) was not taken from him by the Roman Empire, because it belonged to the Father God. Jesus is prepared for that moment, because he is satisfied with his own pen-ultimacy before the Father who is ultimately trustworthy.

This yielding stands in sharp contrast to so much of our society in which we try to fend off death in every way we can. I think we do that, because we do not trust the Father God:

- We fend off death by our inordinate passion for exercise and diet.

- We fend off death by cosmetics that will keep us young and handsome, and I will not even mention Viagra.

- We fend off death by accumulation of more money or property or influence, as if we can make ourselves more secure.

- We fend off death by being right. Whether we are liberal or conservative, we believe we have the final answer, and we find other opinions to be alien and surely mistaken.

- We fend off death by our drive to self-sufficiency, whether it comes in the form of arrogance, anger, or greed.

We do not in our society, commend ourselves over to the Father, but we want to keep ourselves for ourselves on our own terms. Unlike Jesus, we imagine that we are ultimate, and there is no fall-back beneath us.

Jesus yields because he is deeply situated in the piety of his Jewish tradition. In Psalm 31 the Psalm perhaps on the lips of Jesus, describes his life under threat with "terror all around." And then in verses 14–16:

> But I trusted in you, O LORD;
>> I say, "You are my God."
> My times are in your hand;
>> deliver me from the hand of my enemies and
>> persecutors.
> Let your face shine on your servant;
>> save me in your steadfast love. (vv. 14–16)

This must have been how it was for Jesus in that final moment of yielding. After stating the big trouble, he said, "But . . . Nevertheless." Contrary to all the evidence of that violence and mockery around the cross, he can say "nevertheless." Nevertheless I trust you, O Lord. I trust you finally against all the evidence of the power of death.

I say, You are my God.

You are the one to whom I cried, "My God, My God, why have you forsaken me." And then the Psalm says,

> My times are in your hand.

What better!?

This God may have the whole world in his hands. But what counts is that my times are in your hands,, my times of well-being, my times of obedience, my times of joy, but also my times of grief and despair and failure, my times of death, especially my time of dying, are in your hand. The psalm says, it is all in God's hand. And Jesus says, into your hand I commend my life. The hand is image of power. My times are in your power. I commend my life to your power. In this utterance, the Psalmist acknowledges that he is pen-ultimate, that it does not fully depend on him, and that he can confidently relinquish very self to God who has given me breath in the first place. And then, with such yielding in the Psalm, he voices a petition:

> Deliver me from the hand of my enemies and persecutors.

> Let your face shine on your servant.

> Save me in our steadfast love.

And he breathed his last, having yielded his life.

Luke reports three responses to this confident yielding to the Father:

- The soldier guarding the cross, representative of the Roman Empire, watches his death, his violet state execution and declares:

> Certainly this man was innocent.

Or as you know, other gospel witnesses have him say, "This was God's son." The soldier noticed that yielding to the Father in that moment of death was very different from the frightened posturing of the empire.

- The crowds that wanted him executed and said "Crucify him," "beat their breasts." They did so because it became clear that they had urged the execution of an innocent man; they had engaged in mob rage in mindless support of the empire and its self-serving ideology.

- And his followers, not least the women, "watched these things." They could not easily compute what was happening, but they knew that something momentous and unprecedented was happening before their very eyes.

We are also witnesses to this trusting relinquishment of life to the Father.

- We are partly the empire and its soldiers, recognizing who he was, but too late.

- We are partly the crowd, shrinking away in cowardice, because we too often want to eliminate for force of the will of the Father.

- We are among his followers, bewildered by his death, moved by his courage and his freedom.

    And we hear the words of the Psalm:

    Our times are in your hand.

We may consider, In whose hands are our times? The hand of fear, of greed, of anger, of guilt, of cowardice? Or the hands of love, mercy, and justice?

Into Your Hand

We might put our times in God's hand, and then trust our life, our spirit, our breath to the Father who gives us all that we have and all that we are. The narrative in Luke leaves us with Joseph of Arimathea to bury the body. It is said of him, he was "waiting expectantly for the Kingdom of God" (Luke 23:51).

For Further Reading
and Reflection

Allen, Ronald J., and Clark Williamson. *Preaching the Old Testament: A Lectionary Commentary*. Louisville: Westminster John Knox, 2007.

Bartlett, David L., and Barbara Brown Taylor, editors. *Feasting on the Word*. 12 vols. Preaching the Revised Common Lectionary. Louisville: Westminster John Knox, 2011.

Boff, Leonardo. *Passion of Christ, Passion of the World: The Facts, Their Interpretation, and Their Meaning Yesterday and Today*. Translated by Robert R. Barr. Maryknoll, NY: Orbis, 2011.

Brown, Raymond E. *The Gospel of John*. 2 vols. Anchor Bible 29, 29A. Garden City, NY: Doubleday, 1966–1970.

Brueggemann, Walter. *The Collected Sermons of Walter Brueggemann*. Louisville: Westminster John Knox, 2011.

———. *Finally Comes the Poet: Daring Speech for Proclamation*. Minneapolis: Fortress, 1989.

———. *The Practice of Prophetic Imagination: Preaching an Emancipatory Word*. Minneapolis: Fortress, 2012.

———. *The Word Militant: Preaching a Decentering Word*. Minneapolis: Fortress, 2007.

Brueggemann, Walter, Charles B. Cousar, Beverly Gaventa, and James D. Newsome. *Texts for Preaching: A Lectionary Commentary Based on the NRSV*. Vol. 1, *Year A*. Louisville: Westminster John Knox, 1995.

———. *Texts for Preaching: A Lectionary Commentary Based on the NRSV*. Vol. 2, *Year B*. Louisville: Westminster John Knox, 1993.

Cassidy, Sheila. *Good Friday People*. Maryknoll, NY: Orbis, 1991.

For Further Reading and Reflection

Cousar, Beverly Gaventa, and James D. Newsome. *Texts for Preaching: A Lectionary Commentary Based on the NRSV*. Vol. 3, Year C. Louisville: Westminster John Knox, 1994.

Craddock, Fred B., John H. Hayes, Carl R. Holladay, and Gene M. Tucker. *Preaching through the Christian Year: A Comprehensive Commentary on the Lectionary*. 3 vols. Philadelphia: Trinity, 1992.

Florence, Anna Carter. *Preaching as Testimony*. Louisville: Westminster John Knox, 2007.

———. *The Word in Rehearsal*. The Lyman Beecher Lectures in Preaching. Louisville: Westminster John Knox, forthcoming.

Fuller, Reginald H., and Daniel Westberg. *Preaching the Lectionary: The Word of God for the Church Today*. 3rd ed. Collegeville, MN: Liturgical, 2006.

Hall, Douglas John. *The Cross in Our Context: Jesus and the Suffering of the World*. Minneapolis: Fortress, 2003.

Hengel, Martin. *Cross of the Son of God*. Translated by John Bowden. London: SCM, 1986.

Jarvis, Cynthia A., and E. Elizabeth Johnson, editors. *Feasting on the Gospels: A Feasting on the Word Commentary*. Louisville: Westminster John Knox, 2013–.

Lombardo, Nicholas E. *The Father's Will: Christ's Crucifixion and the Goodness of God*. Oxford: Oxford University Press, 2013.

Long, Kimberly Bracken, editor. *Feasting on the Word Worship Companion: Liturgies for Year A*. Vol. 1, *Advent through Pentecost*. Louisville: Westminster John Knox, 2013.

———. *Feasting on the Word Worship Companion: Liturgies for Year A*. Vol. 2, *Trinity Sunday through Reign of Christ*. Louisville: Westminster John Knox, 2013.

———. *Feasting on the Word Worship Companion: Liturgies for Year C*. Vol. 1, *Advent through Pentecost*. Louisville: Westminster John Knox, 2012.

———. *Feasting on the Word Worship Companion: Liturgies for Year C*. Vol. 2, *Trinity Sunday through Reign of Christ*. Louisville: Westminster John Knox, 2012.

McCarroll, Pamela. *Waiting at the Foot of the Cross: Toward a Theology of Hope for Today*. Distinguished Dissertations in Christian Theology 11. Eugene, OR: Pickwick Publications, 2014.

Ruge-Jones, Philip. *Cross in Tensions: Luther's Theology of the Cross as Theologico-Social Critique*. Princeton Theological Monograph Series 92. Eugene, OR: Pickwick Publications, 2008.

Sloyan, Gerard S. *The Crucifixion of Jesus: History, Myth, Faith*. Minneapolis: Fortress, 1995.

For Further Reading and Reflection

————. *Preaching from the Lectionary: An Exegetical Commentary.* Minneapolis: Fortress, 2004.

————. *Why Jesus Died.* Facets. Minneapolis: Fortress, 2004.

Ward, Hannah, and Jennifer Wild, comp. *Resources for Preaching and Worship. Year A: Quotations, Meditations, Poetry, and Prayers.* Louisville: Westminster John Knox, 2004.

————. *Resources for Preaching and Worship. Year B: Quotations, Meditations, Poetry, and Prayers.* Louisville: Westminster John Knox, 2002.

————. *Resources for Preaching and Worship. Year C: Quotations, Meditations, Poetry, and Prayers.* Louisville: Westminster John Knox, 2003.

Recent Works by
Walter Brueggemann

The Practice of Homefulness. Edited by K. C. Hanson. Eugene, OR: Cascade Books, 2014.

With William H. Bellinger Jr. *Psalms.* New Cambridge Bible Commentary. New York: Cambridge University Press, 2014.

Reality, Grief, Hope: Three Urgen Prophetic Tasks. Grand Rapids: Eerdmans, 2014.

Embracing the Transformation. Edited by K. C. Hanson. Eugene, OR: Cascade Books, 2013.

Truth Speaks to Power: The Countercultural Nature of Scripture. Louisville: Westminster John Knox, 2013.

Remember You Are Dust. Edited by K. C. Hanson. Eugene, OR: Cascade Books, 2012.

The Practice of Prophetic Imagination: Preaching an Emancipatory Word. Minneapolis: Fortress, 2012.

With Carolyn Sharpe. *Living Countertestimony: Conversations with Walter Brueggemann.* Louisville: Westminster John Knox, 2012.

With Tod Linafelt. *An Introduction to the Old Testament: The Canon and Christian Imagination.* 2nd ed. Louisville: Westminster John Knox, 2012.

Truth-telling as Subversive Obedience. Edited by K. C. Hanson. Eugene, OR: Cascade Books, 2011.

David and His Theologian: Literary, Social, and Theological Investigations of the Early Monarchy. Edited by K. C. Hanson. Eugene, OR: Cascade Books, 2011.

The Collected Sermons of Walter Brueggemann. Louisville: Westminster John Knox, 2011.

Recent Works by Walter Brueggemann

Disruptive Grace: Reflections on God, Scripture, and the Church. Minneapolis: Fortress, 2011.

Journey to the Common Good. Louisville: Westminster John Knox, 2010.

Out of Babylon. Nashville: Abingdon, 2010.

Divine Presence amid Violence: Contextualizing the Book of Joshua. Eugene, OR: Cascade Books, 2009.

Great Prayers of the Old Testament. Louisville: Westminster John Knox, 2008.

A Pathway of Interpretation: The Old Testament for Pastors and Students. Eugene, OR: Cascade Books, 2008.

Prayers for a Privileged People. Nashville: Abingdon, 2008.

Old Testament Theology: An Introduction. Library of Biblical Theology. Nashville: Abingdon, 2008.

Prayers for a Privileged People. Nashville: Abingdon, 2008.

Praying the Psalms: Engaging Scripture and the Life of the Spirit. 2nd ed. Eugene, OR: Cascade Books, 2007.

The Word Militant: Preaching a Decentering Word. Minneapolis: Fortress, 2007.

Mandate to Difference: An Invitation to the Contemporary Church. Louisville: Westminster John Knox, 2007.

The Word that Redescribes the World: The Bible and Discipleship. Edited by Patrick D. Miller. Minneapolis: Fortress, 2006.

Inscribing the Word: Sermons and Prayers of Walter Brueggemann. Edited by Anna Carter Florence. Minneapolis: Fortress, 2004.

Theology of the Old Testament: Testimony, Dispute, Advocacy. Minneapolis: Fortress, 1997.